STEM IN THE
DAYTONA 500

BY MARNE VENTURA

CONTENT CONSULTANT

JESSE WILCOX, PHD
ASSISTANT PROFESSOR OF STEM EDUCATION
SIMPSON COLLEGE

SportsZone

An Imprint of Abdo Publishing
abdobooks.com

ABDOBOOKS.COM

Published by Abdo Publishing, a division of ABDO, PO Box 398166, Minneapolis, Minnesota 55439. Copyright © 2020 by Abdo Consulting Group, Inc. International copyrights reserved in all countries. No part of this book may be reproduced in any form without written permission from the publisher. SportsZone™ is a trademark and logo of Abdo Publishing.

Printed in the United States of America, North Mankato, Minnesota
102019
012020

Cover Photo: Russell LaBounty/NPK/AP Images
Interior Photos: RacingOne/ISC Images & Archives/Getty Images, 4–5; Racing Photo Archives/Getty Images Sport Classic/Getty Images, 7; Shutterstock Images, 8, 23, 43; Action Sports Photography/Shutterstock Images, 11, 12–13, 19, 20–21; John Raoux/AP Images, 14; Glenn Smith/AP Images, 16; Jared C. Tilton/Getty Images Sports/Getty Images, 24; Phelan M. Ebenhack/AP Images, 27, 36–37; Gary McCullough/Shutterstock Images, 28–29; Nigel Kinrade/NKP/AP Images, 31; Bill Friel/AP Images, 32; iStockphoto, 35; David Graham/AP Images, 39; Red Line Editorial, 40; Wilfredo Lee/AP Images, 44

Editor: Marie Pearson
Series Designer: Dan Peluso

LIBRARY OF CONGRESS CONTROL NUMBER: 2019941986

PUBLISHER'S CATALOGING-IN-PUBLICATION DATA
Names: Ventura, Marne, author.
Title: STEM in the Daytona 500 / by Marne Ventura
Description: Minneapolis, Minnesota : Abdo Publishing, 2020 | Series: STEM in the greatest sports events | Includes online resources and index.
Identifiers: ISBN 9781532190544 (lib. bdg.) | ISBN 9781644943120 (pbk.) | ISBN 9781532176395 (ebook)
Subjects: LCSH: Daytona 500 (Automobile race)--Juvenile literature. | Sports sciences--Juvenile literature. | Applied science--Juvenile literature. | Automobile racing--Juvenile literature. | Physics--Juvenile literature.
Classification: DDC 796.015--dc23

TABLE OF CONTENTS

David Pearson (21) leads the field during a caution lap in the 1976 Daytona 500.

CHAPTER 1

THE GREAT AMERICAN RACE

Stock cars zoomed around the track at an average of 152 miles per hour (245 km/h). It was the last fourth of the 1976 Daytona 500. There were 12 out of 200 laps left to go. David Pearson and Richard Petty had traded off first and second place for 45 of the previous 46 laps. Petty's red Dodge passed Pearson's white Mercury on lap 188. Some 125,000 fans cheered as the drivers rounded the turn.

Pearson drove close behind Petty to get enough speed to pass him as they moved into Turn 3. The momentum of the pass made Pearson's car move up the side of the track. This let Petty slide to the inside of the track. He edged ahead of Pearson again.

The two cars flew side by side around Turn 4. Petty drifted up the track as he sped out of the turn. His car bumped Pearson's. Both cars crashed into the wall. Petty spun, crossed the track, and stalled on the infield. He was just 75 feet (23 m) short of the finish line. He tried in vain to restart his engine.

Meanwhile, Pearson spun, crossed the track, and rolled into the infield too. In the smoke and confusion, Pearson couldn't see Petty. He radioed his crew. They told him Petty was stalled nearby. Pearson's engine was still running. He headed for the finish line. The crumpled car would only go 30 miles per hour (48 km/h). Smoke streamed from the hood. Torn metal scraped against the track. Slowly, Pearson crossed the line and won the race.

Pearson limps toward the finish line while Petty is stuck in the grass.

Petty's crew ran from the pit. They pushed their car across the line. According to National Association for Stock Car Racing (NASCAR) rules, they lost one lap for pushing the car. But because the third-place car was a lap behind, Petty still came in second. The end of the eighteenth Daytona 500 race was one of the most thrilling moments in the history of the event.

Daytona International Speedway has undergone a lot of changes since it opened in 1959.

STEM IN ACTION

The Daytona 500 is the main event of the NASCAR season. Drivers complete 200 laps around the 2.5-mile (4-km) oval track. This totals 500 miles (805 km), and that's why it's called the Daytona 500. The first race was held at Daytona International Speedway in Daytona Beach, Florida, in February 1959. Since then, the race has become one of the most popular sporting events in the United States. Science, technology, engineering, and math (STEM) come into play in every part of the Daytona 500.

Understanding the science of physics helps drivers keep their cars on the track as they turn. They know how to get a little extra speed as they follow the car ahead. They use momentum to then pass that car. Physics also helps crew chiefs choose fuel and tires to keep the car balanced. Chemistry helps them know how to keep tire pressure just right.

Some 9.2 million viewers watched the Daytona 500 on television in 2019. New technologies make viewing better every year. A robotic camera on a rail gives viewers a feel for how fast the cars go. Cameras show the race from all angles. Drones fly overhead to capture the action.

To start, a stock car might look like a family car. Engineers modify the car to keep the driver safe in a high-speed crash. Fire suits protect drivers from heat and flames. Ear protection is essential since the cars don't have mufflers. Crew chiefs rely on engineering to keep the car on the track as it turns.

NASCAR team members are math experts. Drivers and officials keep track of laps and stages to determine the winner. Crew members use numbers to measure and increase the power and speed of their cars. They measure weight and angles to get the best performance and win the race.

Science, technology, engineering, and math have come a long way since the first Daytona 500 in 1959. Over the years, advances in STEM fields have helped make this popular event the Great American Race.

NASCAR teams must understand STEM concepts in order to win the Daytona 500.

NASCAR teams use science to design a car that can race around Daytona International Speedway at high speeds.

CHAPTER **2**

THE SCIENCE OF SPEED

Daytona International Speedway is a tri-oval track. Unlike regular ovals, it has three corners. Crew members and drivers use science to design and drive their cars to work on the speedway. They know how to draft, pass, turn, and stay balanced to win.

The track at Daytona has a very steep slope on the turns. This slope allows stock cars to take the turns at a high speed. To keep speeds safe, NASCAR requires drivers to put restrictor plates on the engines.

The team behind a NASCAR driver is important to the driver's success. A good crew chief is familiar with all of the science behind racing and can make quick, smart decisions.

These plates reduce air and fuel flowing to the engine.

This prevents the cars from going too dangerously fast.

Top speeds average 200 miles per hour (320 km/h).

DRAFTING, PASSING, AND TURNING

NASCAR teams have found another way to kick up speed. It's called drafting. A speeding stock car is hit by air molecules. They push against the front of the car in the opposite direction the car is heading. This slows it down. This is called drag. As the car moves forward, it creates a pocket of low air pressure behind it. This slows the car by pulling it backward. NASCAR drivers use drafting to solve both of these problems. One driver gets just inches behind the car ahead. The air molecules move over both cars as if they were one car. This creates less drag on the second car. At the same time, the car behind fills the low-pressure area made by the first car. There is less backward pull on the first car. Drafting causes both cars to go 3 to 5 miles per hour (5 to 8 km/h) faster than they would on their own.

While drafting helps the car behind go faster, its driver still needs to get ahead in order to win. This is where passing comes into play. A skilled driver in the

———————————▶ Low-Pressure Air

———————————▶ Medium-Pressure Air

———————————▶ High-Pressure Air

Drivers increase speed by drafting. Air molecules traveling
over the car in front continue over the second car. This
decreases drag for the car behind. The second car fills the
low-pressure space behind the first car. This also decreases
drag for the first car.

REDUCING DRAG

car behind knows how to speed up when approaching a turn. Entering the turn, the driver can burst out from behind and shoot past the car in front. This is called a slingshot.

Turning is the trickiest part of driving at the speedway. Making smart moves in the corners is how drivers win the race. When a car is moving straight at 180 miles per hour (290 km/h), it takes 10,000 pounds (4,500 kg) of force to get the car into and out of a turn. On a speedway, the force comes from the interaction between the tires, the track, and the air. The corners of the speedway are as steep as a ski slope. As the sloped track pushes against the tires, it creates force that turns

MODIFICATIONS

NASCAR teams modify their cars to get rid of rough surfaces or parts that stick out. They place side view mirrors just inside the car. They cover most of the grille with tape. These changes help reduce drag because there are fewer parts to bump into air molecules.

the car, keeps it on the track, and builds speed. Air pushing sideways on the car helps it turn too.

BALANCE

Tire pressure is an important tool for winning the Daytona 500. Friction between the tire and the track causes tires to heat up during the race. When gas molecules inside the tire heat up, they move faster. They hit the inside wall of the tire and push outward. This builds tire pressure. To keep tire pressure from getting too high, NASCAR crews use nitrogen instead of air from the atmosphere in their tires. Air has nitrogen, but also oxygen, water vapor, and other gases. Nitrogen is a gas that doesn't build as much pressure as air. Air from the atmosphere could build up too much pressure, causing the tires to pop more easily.

A winning NASCAR team carefully plans the car's center of gravity. This is the balance point of a car. If you picked a car up with a crane at the center of gravity, the car would hang perfectly level. If the crane attached to

Pit stops are carefully timed to help the car perform its best at key moments in the race.

a spot just a bit away from that spot, the car would hang at an angle. When the weight of the race car pushes the tires against the track, it creates grip. This force holds the tires on the track. During a race, the tires wear down. At the same time, the car is burning fuel. The fuel tank at the rear of the car becomes lighter. The car's center of gravity shifts forward. This also changes the grip of the tires. To keep a car balanced, crews change tires and refuel cars during pit stops.

More than 100,000 fans pack the grandstands each year to watch the Daytona 500.

3

TECHNOLOGY ON THE TRACK

Daytona International Speedway seats 101,500 fans. The race is usually sold out every year. Millions of other fans watch the race on TV. New advances in technology let camera operators and TV broadcasters help fans experience the event no matter where they are.

A high-speed camera tracking system was used at the Daytona 500 for the first time in 2019. Cameras at sporting events are usually mounted on a dolly. This base with wheels lets the operator move the camera while filming. The dolly is attached to a track that is 850 feet (259 m) long. It was installed behind the inside wall of Turn 2.

A camera mounted on the track, called the rail cam, moves in response to commands from a computer system. If a car comes out of a turn going 180 mph (290 km/h), the camera might move 80 miles per hour (130 km/h) in the same direction as car. Other times, the camera moves 80 miles per hour (130 km/h) toward the car that's coming out of the turn at 180 miles per hour (290 km/h). This helps fans experience the speed of the car from close up, as if they were on the track.

PIT STOP ACTION

Part of the excitement of the Daytona 500 is seeing how quickly the crew works during a pit stop. Camera operators at sports events normally use a jib. A jib is a long arm that acts like a seesaw. The arm has a camera mounted on one end. The other end holds a weight. The jib is attached to a tripod near the weighted end.

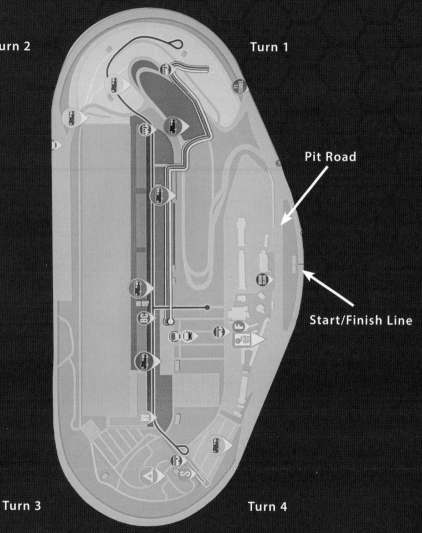

Turn 2

Turn 1

Pit Road

Start/Finish Line

Turn 3

Turn 4

Television camera crews mount the high-speed rail cam on the inside of Turn 2. Pit road, at the third corner of the tri-oval near the start and finish line, is where cars stop for tire changes and refueling. Camera operators wearing body jibs photograph pit crews from inside the pit.

Body jibs allow camera operators the ability to give viewers up-close shots of pit stop action without getting in the way of the pit crews.

This device allows the camera operator to get the camera close to the subject. It lets the operator move the camera from a distance. At the Daytona 500, an operator wears the jib on his or her body. The weight of the operator's body balances the weight of the camera at the other end. Stationed in the pit box, these body-jib operators can get the camera above the car or down on the ground beside it. They can film the action of the pit stop so that viewers feel like they are there.

CAMERAS EVERYWHERE

At the 2019 Daytona 500, a drone made history. A drone is a flying robot. Drones carrying cameras have been used to film sporting events before. The drones are attached to cables that run above the field. But the drone at the 2019 event was a first because it had no cable. A licensed pilot flew the drone. In addition to being free of cables, the drone was the first to send the video it recorded straight to the production team, which showed the video on live TV. For safety reasons, the pilot could only fly the drone over areas where no fans were seated. He was also not allowed to fly it over the track during the race. He had to fly it off to the side of the track where there were no fans. Although it's rare for a drone to fall out of the sky, officials didn't want to take a chance that it might hit a spectator or a speeding car.

Television viewers can also see the race from inside a speeding stock car. At the 2019 Daytona 500, a camera was mounted on the helmet of one of the drivers. There were also 14 in-car cameras at the race, more than at any NASCAR race for the past 15 years. For the past 10 years, television broadcasters have buried tiny cameras in the asphalt track surface. There is one in Turn 4 and another in the backstretch. The cameras show the cars speeding over the track at more than 200 miles per hour (320 km/h).

3-D GRAPHICS

New technology lets television broadcasters place special computer-generated pictures, words, and numbers over the video of stock cars speeding around turns at the speedway. For example, one video shows a car being pulled apart so the viewers can see what makes it work on the inside.

Cameras attached to cables speed over the Daytona track to film the race.

Careful engineering is important to protect drivers in high-speed crashes.

CHAPTER

4

ENGINEERING SAFE SPEED

Acar speeding out of a turn at the Daytona 500 has kinetic energy. The faster it moves, the more kinetic energy it has. Energy can't be made or destroyed. It can only be changed from one form to another. When a car crashes, it won't slow down and stop until all of its kinetic energy changes to other forms of energy. The car spins and heats up. It crashes, and some kinetic energy gets transferred to the wall, road, other cars, or the grass and soil. Metal crumples and tears. This kinetic energy of the car in motion changes into the energy of its metal tearing, crumpling, and heating up.

NASCAR teams design cars with energy in mind. There are three parts to a stock car. The front and rear of the car are made of materials that will bend or crush. The center of the car, where the driver sits, is made of steel tubing. This is more solid and less flexible than the front and rear materials. The driver's seat is custom fitted to keep the driver stable. During a crash, the crumple zones in the front and back of the car absorb

EAR PROTECTION

The Daytona 500 is very loud. It's important that fans and drivers wear ear protection. Earplugs and earmuffs are two kinds of hearing protection. Sound travels in waves. The higher the peaks and dives of the wave, the louder the sound. Earplugs and earmuffs are made with materials such as foam that help block sound waves. They make noises sound quieter. Earplugs create a seal inside the ear canal so sound waves have to pass through the plugs. Earmuffs create a seal around the ear.

NASCAR drivers such as Danica Patrick wear fire suits and gloves, as well as special helmets.

kinetic energy as the car slows down and stops. The driver stays safe while these parts are torn or crushed.

HEAT

Gasoline fire is a danger for NASCAR drivers. Drivers wear fire suits made from a special fiber called Nomex that doesn't melt or burn. It's made with three layers.

Neither Juan Pablo Montoya nor the truck's driver were injured in the fiery crash.

Air between the layers helps stop the transfer of heat. If the outer layer reaches 1,800 degrees Fahrenheit (980°C), it forms a shell of carbon. The shell stops the fire from using the fabric underneath as fuel. The shell also makes the suit thicker so it's harder for flames to get through.

These suits can protect a driver in a fire, but only for five seconds. So drivers still have to hurry to get away from a burning car.

In 2012, officials called for a caution period with 40 laps to go. Juan Pablo Montoya suddenly lost control of his car. It slid into a truck that was drying the track. That truck held up to 200 gallons (760 L) of jet fuel. There was an immediate explosion. Fuel poured onto the track and burned hot. Montoya had trained to get out of his car quickly, and he escaped unharmed. But his clothing also protected him. He could feel the heat of the blaze as he made his escape.

LOAD TRANSFER

Engineers design cars to have good grip. Without grip, tires will slip, slide, spin, or even rise up from the track. A car's center of gravity affects its grip. It is usually near the driver's seat. That's where it will best help the car turn quickly. The weight balanced at the driver's seat helps the left tires grip the road as the car turns.

The body of a race car is connected to the wheels by springs. The wheels are always touching the ground. When speeding cars go into a turn, the weight shifts. The body of the car moves on its springs. This changes how much weight is pushing down on each tire. As a driver brakes and enters a left turn, the weight shifts from the rear wheels to the front wheels, and from the left wheels to the right wheels. When the driver speeds up, the weight shifts from the front wheels to the rear wheels. These weight shifts allow the wheels to remain stable and keep an even grip while speeding around a turn. Without springs, the car might slide, slip, roll, or crash.

Engineers try to get the center of gravity of a race car as close to the ground as possible. This helps cars keep good grip with all four tires. Less weight shifts from one place to another when the center of gravity is low. Engineers lower the center of gravity by placing weights in the lower part of the car.

High Center of Gravity

Car tips on its side

Low Center of Gravity

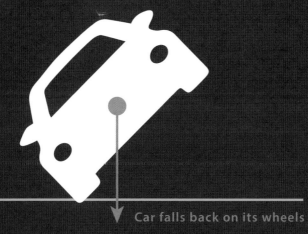

Car falls back on its wheels

A car with a lower center of gravity is stabler than a car with a higher center of gravity. It takes a steeper angle to make a car with a low center of gravity roll over. Engineers add weight to the lower halves of race cars to make them stabler.

With 40 to 43 cars in the race, finishing second like Darrell Wallace Jr. did in 2018 is an achievement worth celebrating.

WINNING WITH MATH

Numbers are used to measure every aspect of NASCAR. Officials count laps to determine the winners. NASCAR teams use math to measure the power and speed of their engines. Math helps NASCAR crews keep their speeding cars on the track as they cross the finish line.

NASCAR divides the Daytona 500 race into three parts called stages. This format was introduced at the 2017 race. Stage 1 and Stage 2 are 60 laps each. Stage 3 is

80 laps. NASCAR officials wave a flag over the start and finish line to signal the drivers. A green flag means go and is used to start each stage. A yellow flag signals caution. A caution might be needed when an accident occurs and a stalled car or car parts need to be cleared away. A green-and-white checkered flag signals the end of a stage. A white flag means there is one lap left in the race. The last flag to be waved is the black-and-white checkered flag. It signals the end of the race. The first driver to cross the finish line at the end of Stage 3 is the winner of the Daytona 500.

HORSEPOWER

One unit of horsepower equals the power needed to lift 330 pounds (150 kg) for a distance of 100 feet (30 m) in one minute. Stock cars at the Daytona 500 have 850 horsepower. This means they can lift or pull more than 140 tons (130 metric tons)—the weight of a blue whale—a distance of 100 feet (30 m) in one minute.

After counting down 200 laps, the black-and-white checkered flag tells drivers they have crossed the finish line.

MEASURING POWER

It takes a lot of power to be the winner. Power is how fast the engine can change the energy in the fuel into speed at the wheels. NASCAR teams use math to figure out how to get more power. Engineers measure the power of an engine with units called horsepower.

Algebra can describe the relationship between the revolutions per minute (RPM) of a wheel and the speed of a stock car.

The equation is:

$$\frac{\text{distance by minute (how far the wheel travels)}}{\text{circumference of the wheel}} = \text{RPM}$$

At 120 miles per hour, the car is moving 2 miles (3.2 km) per minute. A mile is 5,280 feet (1,609 m). So the distance the car has traveled is 10,560 feet (3,219 m) per minute. The equation for the circumference of a wheel in feet is:

pi x diameter in feet $=$ circumference

NASCAR wheels are 1.25 feet (0.38 m) in diameter.

3.1416 x 1.25 $=$ 3.927 feet

$$\frac{10{,}560 \text{ feet per minute}}{3.927 \text{ feet}} = \text{RPM} = 2{,}689 \text{ RPM}$$

A normal car has 150 to 200 horsepower. Stock cars at the Daytona 500 have 850 horsepower. Horsepower is generated when the mixture of fuel and air make an explosion, called combustion, in the engine. This causes the wheels to turn. NASCAR engineers create more horsepower by spinning the engine at a higher speed. The spinning of the engine is measured in revolutions per minute (RPMs). The more combustion events there are, the higher the RPMs and the faster the wheels turn. Most NASCAR engines run at 9,500 RPMs. A family car might run at 2,500 RPMs.

DOWNFORCE AND ANGLES

Downforce helps cars grip the track. Downforce comes from the weight of the car and the air molecules pushing against the car. According to NASCAR rules, cars cannot weigh less than 3,400 pounds (1,540 kg). An average NASCAR stock car weighs 3,450 pounds (1,560 kg). While the weight of the car helps create grip, too much weight causes extra friction. Too much friction can slow down a car.

Air molecules also add to downforce. Daniel Bernoulli was a Swiss mathematician. He is known for a formula called Bernoulli's principle. It explains how the movement of air works. Slow-moving air has more force than air moving quickly. That is because it is denser. A car pushing into slow-moving air runs into more air molecules. Engineers put a splitter on the front of the car. The shelf-like device is below the grill and reaches horizontally just above the track. It splits the flow of air molecules. The air that goes above the splitter hits the front of the car and slows down. This creates a high-pressure region. It pushes down on the splitter. The air that goes under the car moves quickly so it has low pressure. Since there is less air beneath the car, the molecules above the splitter push the car down.

On the back of the car, engineers attach a spoiler. This is a panel that extends up from the back hood of

Spoiler

Splitter

Math explains the need for splitters and spoilers.

the car. Air hits the spoiler, slows, and is forced up and over it. The spoiler is 8 inches (20 cm) high. A steep angle on the spoiler gives more surface area for air to push against as it travels over the wing. This increases the downforce on the back of the car. Air molecules travel quickly. When a car moving at 180 miles per hour (290 km/h) hits these molecules, a lot of downforce

STEM concepts play an important role in the Daytona 500.

is created. NASCAR engineers use math to take advantage of this downforce.

ENJOYING THE RACE

People are always learning new things in the fields of science, technology, engineering, and math. New knowledge will continue to shape the Daytona 500 in the future. Knowing about how STEM influences the great race can make the event even more exciting for fans. And it can give competitors a winning edge.

GLOSSARY

draft
To drive inches behind a race car in order to increase speed.

drag
A force that slows motion.

drifted
Moved slightly without trying.

force
A push or pull that causes movement.

friction
Resistance that happens when one object rubs against another.

gravity
A force that pulls things toward a massive object such as Earth.

grip
The force that keeps a car's tires on the track.

kinetic
Having to do with motion.

molecules
Small parts of a thing.

momentum
A combination of speed in a certain direction and mass.

pit
A sunken area where crew members wait to service race cars.

MORE INFORMATION

BOOKS

Marquardt, Meg. *STEM in Auto Racing*. Minneapolis, MN: Abdo Publishing, 2018.

Rule, Heather. *Ultimate NASCAR Road Trip*. Minneapolis, MN: Abdo Publishing, 2019.

INDEX

ABOUT THE AUTHOR

Marne Ventura is the author of many books for kids, both fiction and nonfiction. She enjoys writing about science, technology, engineering and math, arts and crafts, and the lives of creative people. A former elementary school teacher, she holds a master's degree in education from the University of California. Marne and her husband live on the central coast of California.